animal babies

about the house

KINGFISHER

Kingfisher Publications Plc
New Penderel House
283–288 High Holborn
London WC1V 7HZ
www.kingfisherpub.com

First published by Kingfisher Publications Plc 2005
10 9 8 7 6 5 4 3 2 1

1TR/1204/TWP/SGCH(SGCH)/150STORA/C

Copyright © Kingfisher Publications Plc 2005

A CIP catalogue record for this book is available from the British Library.

ISBN–13: 978 0 7534 1077 6
ISBN–10: 0 7534 1077 X

Author and Editor: Vicky Weber
Designer: Joanne Brown
Proofreader: Jennifer Schofield
Picture Research Manager: Cee Weston-Baker
Picture Researcher: Rachael Swann
DTP Manager: Nicky Studdart
Senior Production Controller: Lindsey Scott

Printed in Singapore

animal babies

about the house

I am good at climbing and jumping. I can race up trees in seconds and leap down from fences.

Who is my mummy?

My mummy is a cat and I am her kitten.

I look just like my daddy. He also has a black and white coat.

I live in water and swim round and round all day. When I am older my scaly skin will turn deep gold.

Who is my mummy?

My mummy is a goldfish and I am her fry.

We breathe through flaps of skin near our eyes called gills.

When I am in a good mood and want to play, I wag my tail and bark as loudly as I can.

Who is my mummy?

My mummy is a dog and I am her puppy.

We have lots of energy and love to run around outside in the garden.

I love to eat fruit. If you peel an orange, I will smell it and hope that you share it with me.

Who is my mummy?

My **mummy** is a guinea pig and I am her **pup**.

When we are given **tasty** food, we **squeal** loudly with **excitement**.

I use my large, hooked beak to crack open brazil nuts. My beautiful feathers are a bluey-gold colour.

Who is my mummy?

My **mummy** is a macaw and I am her **baby**.

We like to **copy** some of the **words** you **say**. Talking is great **fun!**

I have big ears that stick up in the air. My hearing is so good that I can tell when another animal is nearby.

Who is my mummy?

My mummy is a rabbit and I am her bunny.

We hop along speedily on our strong back legs.

I have four **short** legs and **clawed** feet. My front teeth grow really long, so I **nibble nuts** to wear them down.

Who is my mummy?

My mummy is a hamster and I am her pup.

We often sleep during the day and are wide awake at night.

Note

All the animals in this book can be kept as pets. If you are thinking of buying a pet, make sure you know what is involved before you make your purchase. All pets need care and attention and many of them can be time consuming. But they also bring a lot of fun and happiness. You should check that it is legal in your country to keep the pet and whether you need a licence for it. These animals might also exist in the wild but if you see a sweet and cuddly animal in the countryside, do not approach it as it might become frightened and attack you.

Acknowledgements

The publisher would like to thank the following for permission to reproduce their material. Every care has been taken to trace copyright holders. However, if there have been unintentional omissions or failure to trace copyright holders, we apologise and will, if informed, endeavour to make corrections in any future edition.

Cover: DiMaggio/Kalish/Corbis; Half title: Heidi and Hans Juergen Koch/Minden/FLPA; Title page: Manfred Danegger/ NHPA; Cat 1: ImageBank/Getty Images; Cat 2: Daniel Heuclin/NHPA; Goldfish 1: Martin Harvey/Alamy; Goldfish 2: Zefa/F.Hirdes; Dog 1: Image Bank/Getty Images; Dog 2: Mitsuaki Iwago/Minden/FLPA; Guinea pig 1: Maximilian Weinzierl/Alamy; Guinea pig 2: Ernie Janes/Sunset/FLPA; Macaw 1: Frans Lanting/Minden/ FLPA; Macaw 2: Kenneth Fink/ardea.com; Rabbit 1: Manfred Danegger/NHPA; Rabbit 2: Manfred Danegger/ NHPA; Hamster 1: Heidi and Hans Juergen Koch/Minden/FLPA; Hamster 2: Heidi and Hans Juergen Koch/Minden/FLPA